Rainbow'

Book of Poetry

Lily Lawson

THE
WRIGHT HOUSE

Cover design
by Ann Garcia

By The Author

Poetry Books

My Fathers Daughter,
A Taste of What's to Come,
Rainbow's Red Book of Poetry
Rainbow's Orange Book of Poetry

Kids' Books

Santa's Early Christmas,
The Palm Tree Swingers Island Band
If I Were Invisible…

Words
just words
and yet
much more.

I bow to the artist,
the poet, the dreamer,
the weaver of words.

I am humbled by your mastery.
I give thanks.

Rainbow's Orange Book of Poetry is the second book in the Rainbow series of seven books, one for each colour of the rainbow.

Orange means passion, and my two passions are music and writing, the constants in my life.

When I was eleven we started to write poetry at school. The poetry I had read up to that point was written in language that was hard to understand. Poets didn't write like we spoke. Then my teacher used the Beatles' song *Yesterday* to inspire us, and music led me to poetry.

I started writing and every time I wandered away from it, something always brought me back. Through poetry, I've learned who I am as a person, expressed my thoughts and emotions, made new connections, and strengthened existing ones.

I believe poetry should speak to us in a way we can relate to. We can say a lot in ordinary words.

I don't write poetry books. I write poems and some of them find their way into books. The theme reveals itself along the way. Poems present themselves; some make the final cut; some will find a new home elsewhere.

Welcome to the poems that found a home in *Orange*.

Contents

Poetry is Alive

I am a poet
It's what I do.
I convey
my words to you
in dancing fire,
in beating drum.
I've finished
before you've begun.

The novelist
of whom you've likely heard
may find
my brevity absurd.
There is space
for a weighty tome,
when you find yourself
at home.

Poetry dances
in the air,
it has the skill
of Fred Astaire.
It finds its way
through tiny nooks,
to people with no time

for books.

It lives and breathes
and can be found
even on the
underground,
graffitied
with a can of paint
or in collections
oh, how quaint.

It is recited oft
by heart
in entirety
or part.
I must insist
we put to bed
the thought of
poetry being dead.

Poets Anonymous

Living, breathing,
expressing ideas
my voice cannot explain.

The poetry I love
speaks to me
in secret code.

Ordinary words,
skilfully arranged,
holding me spellbound.
Clamouring, addicted,
I retrace my steps
to feed again on its mastery.

The poet lives on.
When the last breath
is wrung from the body,
the soul carries the poet's voice.

Journey

Structures that held people
and events that shaped my life,
destroyed, evolved, or laid to waste.
Mere shells of what I once knew them to be.
My past lies littered with them all.

Unnecessary signage,
proclaiming no returns,
doors closing behind me as I go.

Abandoned clothes unfitting
for the person I'll become,
through another door
I have yet to locate,
waiting for me somewhere up ahead.

Gratitude seeps from my every pore,
for those long gone,
or yet to grace my life,
and most of all for those who walk with me.

6

Please Let Me rhyme

I don't always need it.
I used to do it all the time.
Some think that it's essential,
to not use it is a crime.
It may no longer be a constant,
but the choice needs to be mine.
It's not what makes me a poet,
but you have to let me rhyme.

I See You in Your Absorption

Bring me your cold coffee,
your hunger pangs,
your dry throats,
your forgotten houseplants,
your neglected housework,
and I will say,
'Hey writer!'

I Crave My Fix

When you write,
you take ordinary words,
sprinkle them with magic,
touch my soul.

When you write,
you strip away
needless sugar coating,
dragging my emotions into light.

When you write,
I am visiting a place
I haven't been before,
I have no wish to leave.

When you write,
I could become addicted
to your poetic phrasing,
I need more.

World Poetry Day

I weave my secrets into your fine threads,
covering them beyond detection,
allowing me the freedom of expression
without the vulnerability of exposure,
in endless streams.

You accompany my walks in solitude,
offering refuge from the encounters
I would never seek to face.
When human consolation turns its back,
you will remain.

I fill you up with my uncertainty
and my selfish need.
Insecurity may touch you,
but would never find a place
within your walls.

I am beyond the point of gratitude
I have not words enough
to do you justice
to truly express the value,
that I place upon you, in my life.

Poetic Choreography

My words fall onto the page,
knowing their place better than I.

They form their groups,
shifting into position,
to suit each situation.

Adaptable, flexible, ready,
willing to be used.

Expectation of earning their keep,
understood, accepted.

Taking rejection well,
knowing opportunities arise.

The right fit comes with patience.

Their reward the attention they receive.

Poetic Dance

Some poets learn the steps
of a familiar routine,
keeping the rhythm,
hitting every beat.

Some poets know many dances,
utilising their unique talents,
skilfully adapting,
until the music ends.

Some poets express themselves,
free from restraints,
their individual choreography
resulting in surprising outcomes.

Elements

Earth grounds me,
reliable, unshifting, steady, safe,
solid, quietly supportive.

Air lifts me,
unpredictable, fleeting, joy across my skin,
from a whisper to a howl making its voice heard.

Fire empowers me,
passion, desire, motivation, strength,
its aroma stretches beyond its presence.

Water calms me,
Poetic, gentle, subtle, noisy, exuberant, bold,
its universal language understood.

Love Seeks ...

to build
not to destroy,
to comfort
not to injure,
to stand beside
not to abandon,
to walk toward
not to walk away,
to listen
not to ignore,
to accept
not to reject,
to welcome
not to turn away.

I long for your voice
to punctuate my silence.
I recognise my need
is more than you can cope with.
Forgive my intrusion.
The moments I find hard,
you bring light to.
I have yet to accomplish that skill.

Three Words are Enough

Just three words
'I love you.'

Just three words
'Leave me alone.'

Just three words
'How are you?'

Just three words
'I'm coming home.'

Just three words
'I am sorry.'

Just three words
'Thinking of you.'

Just three words
'Make a difference.'

Just three words
'Over to you.'

The Book of Us

An eraser is insufficient to remove the hurtful
words
from my correspondence to you,
written in indelible ink.

No editor could take the pain away.

I am no ghost.
Those words were mine alone.
There's no rewrite,
no second draft.
They remain published in original format.

No matter the word count
the highlights will be referred to
when you review our relationship.

No matter the twists and turns of the plot,
wherever the story ends,
my final chapter will contain the words 'I love you'
even if you never return to my book.

I Don't Understand

You broke me into pieces.
Which I could have forgiven
if you didn't understand,
but you did.

When I'm begging,
you walk without a backward glance.
I tell myself reluctantly,
you are right to leave.

This has run its course.
I move into acceptance.
I no longer need you;
we had become unhealthy.

I carry on and thrive.
Seeking other company
I barely give you a thought
or even reminisce.

Then suddenly you come.
I don't see the point.
Did you leave in haste?
Did regret pave your return?

To my surprise
I don't care anymore.
I'm in a better place.
I want you gone.

I can't become entangled.
After everything, we are
more than acquaintances,
but our friendship's at an end.

Imagining a Poet

Poets in my head
write with quills on parchment,
in a room lit by a lantern,
a fire in the grate.

They pen the words they cannot speak,
their passion fuelled by all-consuming love
for a lover lost, amid dramatic showdowns.

Their broken-hearted lover
is wooed by another love.
Yet none shall replace the poet,
who first stole their heart.

All is not lost until the final couplet,
for love alone may not be enough,
but life without love never is.

Take Time to Listen

Poetry spoke
the language of the long dead,
its curious spelling and strange vocabulary
foreign on my tongue.

It called to me
through intervening years,
a plea from those who penned the lines I read,
that they be understood and so live on
in books that many hands have held,
some with care, some without.

The language
developed and moved on,
a living thing,
adapted in spoken and written form,
so that it may convey the messages of our time
to include or exclude.

I hope
generations yet to be
will listen to the words
of long forgotten use,
and hear the call
of poetry.

Now you've read my book
don't forget to review
Amazon, Goodreads,
Bookbub too!
Thank you very much
I'm counting on you!

Lily x

A Poem from

Rainbow's Red Book of Poetry

Hate vs Love

Hate leaks from lips,
its powerful punch poisoning all within its wake,
wasting weighty words on trivial pursuits.

Love flows from the heart,
its calming lotion pouring in caressing streams,
healing wounds, seeping into souls.

Hate's afflicted admirers
keen to ingratiate themselves
bow and scrape at its feet.
When they hear the battle cry, they charge.

Love listens long.
Its gentle voice persuading, reaching out,
accepting all in its embrace.

Acknowledgements

Thank you for reading my book.

If you hate it tell me, if you love it tell everybody!

Thanks to Ann Garcia for my cover.

Thanks to Cheryl, Alex, Becky, Jo and all who ARCed this book.

Thanks to Cin.

Thanks to all who follow me anywhere and all who put up with my randomness.

Thanks to Butterfly who has taught me so much.

Thanks to my dad for everything.